FRANZ LISZT

Complete Etudes for Solo Piano

SERIES I
Including the Transcendental Etudes

Edited by Ferruccio Busoni

DOVER PUBLICATIONS, INC., *New York*

Published in Canada by General Publishing Company, Ltd.,
30 Lesmill Road, Don Mills, Toronto, Ontario.
Published in the United Kingdom by
Constable and Company, Ltd.

This Dover edition, first published in 1988, is a republication of Vol. 1 and a portion of Vol. 2 (both titled *Etüden für Pianoforte zu zwei Händen*) of Ser. 2 (*Pianofortewerke*) of the set *Franz Liszt's Musikalische Werke herausgegeben von der Franz Liszt-Stiftung*, originally published by Breitkopf & Härtel, Leipzig, n.d. (editor's commentaries dated 1910 and 1911). A table of contents has been added; Rosamond Ley's translation of the Foreword and a new translation of the editorial notes have replaced the original German.

We are grateful to the Paul Klapper Library of Queens College for the loan of the score.

Manufactured in the United States of America
Dover Publications, Inc.
31 East 2nd Street
Mineola, N.Y. 11501

Library of Congress Cataloging-in-Publication Data

Liszt, Franz, 1811–1886.
    [Etudes, piano]
    Complete etudes for solo piano.

    Reprint. Originally published: Musikalische Werke. Leipzig : Breitkopf & Härtel, 1910–1911, (Series II, v. 1–3) With translated introd.
    Contents: ser. 1. Etude en 12 exercices : op. 1, 1826 ; 12 grandes études : 1837 ; Mazeppa : 1840 ; Etudes d'exécution transcendante : 1851—ser. 2. Grande fantaisie de bravoure sur La clochette de Paganini : op. 2, 1832 ; Etudes d'exécution transcendante d'après Paganini : 1838 ; Grandes études de Paganini : — [etc.]
    1. Piano music. I. Busoni, Ferruccio, 1866–1924. II. Title.
M22.L77E83   1988   88-752979
ISBN 0-486-25815-7 (v. 1)
ISBN 0-486-25816-5 (v. 2)

Contents

Foreword

The Studies, the work on which Liszt was occupied from childhood to manhood should, we consider, be put at the head of his pianoforte compositions. There are three reasons for this. The first is that by giving them this position the fact is established that they are thought to be his earliest publication. Liszt's autograph catalogue (Breitkopf & Härtel, 1855), which puts the studies first of all, is the second reason. The third and strongest reason is that the studies in their entirety give, as do no other of his works, the picture of Liszt's pianistic personality in seed, in growth and finally in self-clarification.

These fifty-eight pianoforte pieces alone would place Liszt in the rank of the greatest "pianoforte" composers since Beethoven, Chopin, Schumann, Alkan, Brahms. The collected edition, of which the studies form scarcely the tenth part, will prove that Liszt towers above these composers in his command over pianistic forms.

It will give a picture of him in many lights and in many attitudes and through it we learn to know and to study the sides of his personality which differ most widely—the Mephistophelian and the Religious: he who acknowledges God does not value the Devil less —the sentimental and the inspired. Here you find the acknowledged interpreter of every style, besides the astonishing transformation artist who can wear the costume of any country with the delusive airs of a native. This collected edition will reveal a pianoforte work that draws into its circle the musical compositions of all languages, nations, and epochs from Palestrina to *Parsifal*; Liszt recreated what he took from them—a creator in a double sense.

We witness his transformation from demon to angel from the first *Fantaisie de Bravoure sur la Clochette de Paganini* (on a diabolical suggestion of Paganini's), on to the childlike mysticism of the *Weihnachtsbaum* in which that final simplicity, the fruit of all his experience, sounds strangely from over the border of "a better land." . . .

Here he casts a magic spell and there bewitches, here his aim is to awaken feeling, there to stimulate imagina-tion, and he is always inexhaustible in embellishments. An eye-witness relates how Liszt—pondering over a cadenza—sat down at the piano and tried three or four dozen variations of it, playing each one right through until he had made his choice.

The secret of Liszt's ornamentation is its symmetry. A classic's certainty of form is united with the freedom of improvisation, the harmony of a revolutionary lies within the calm hand of a ruler—the melodic genius of the Latin race flowers above the serious mind of the northerner. Ringing through it all and making every-thing golden is his sense of sound and the piano rules over all, lending wings to the course of his conception; and as Liszt's Idea gives the pianoforte its language, a mutual interplay of happy give and take is created and the boundaries of anticipation and response merge im-perceptibly one into the other.

As interpreter alone Liszt shows the art of keeping the listener's attention on the stretch for points which never fail to appear, and when they appear, never disappoint.

The building and the construction in his Fantasies is inimitable. The distribution of contrasts, the admira-ble choice of characterising moments and motives. And here, also, the pianistically ornamental and non-essen-tial parts of the work, used partly for characterisation and partly in the service of the instrument, are never without their purpose—they, as it were, fill the me-lodic branches with leaves and flowers. The way in which Liszt ennobles the trivial, enlarges the small, pushes forward what is important, and develops what is great, is all shown incontestably in the Fantasies and transcriptions. In this complete edition these take their place as one half, and not the less important one, of Liszt's genius for the pianoforte.

The main substance of this series of Studies consists in the following:

(a) Twelve *Études d'exécution transcendante*
(b) Six *Bravour-Studien nach Paganini*
(c) *Ab-irato*
(d) Three *Études de Concert*
(e) *Waldesrauschen* and *Gnomenreigen*

v

(a) *The Twelve Great Studies*

There are three editions of them and they are all collected here. The first appeared in Frankfurt in 1826. It was furnished with a picture of the young Liszt, a lithograph, which foreshortens the boyish head, and gives him romantic distorted eyes. It is difficult to determine his age from the portrait but it might have been drawn some years before the music was printed. Under it is written: "Franz Liszt, Pianist," and the title page runs:

Étude
pour le Piano-Forte
en quarante-huit exercises
Dans tous les Tons Majeurs et Mineurs
Composées et dediées
à
Mademoiselle Lidie Garella
par
Le jeune Liszt
En quatre Livraisons contenant douze Études chaque
Oeuvre 6
à Paris
chez Dufaut et Dubois, Éditeurs de Musique.
Rue de Gros Chenet No. 2 et Boulevard
Poissonnière No. 10
chez Boisselot Éditeur de Musique
à MARSEILLE
Propriété de Boisselot

It is noticeable that the word *Étude* in the title is in the singular. Further, that the work was planned in forty-eight pieces, and this number should have been the first of four, but it stopped short with this single one. Finally, that it takes the opus number 6. I was able to ascertain, as a matter of fact, that there are two volumes of Variations, op. 1 and 2, which precede these early works, and an Impromptu, op. 3, and *Deux Allegri de Bravoura*, op. 4.

On the other hand there is presumably a fifth opus of which there is no record, and which cannot be found.

That Hofmeister published this self-same volume of Studies as op. 1, shows that it was the first work of Liszt's *published in Germany*.

Hofmeister's edition differs also in the title. This title page, the letters of which are executed in copper print and framed with a kind of lithographic drawing, runs thus:

Études
Pour le
Piano
En douze Exercices
composées
par
F. Liszt
Oeuvre I
Travail de la Jeunesse
Liv. I 16 Gr.   Liv. II, 20 Gr.
Leipsig. Chez Fr. Hofmeister.

The reduction of the forty-eight exercises to twelve and the little tailpiece "youthful work" almost asking for indulgence, points to a later time of publication. I will mention at once the fact that the next printed work of Liszt's *Fantasie über die Braut von Auber* appeared in the year 1829, again with the opus number 1, and that a second (*La Clochette*) soon followed it; the numbers 3 and 4 are not repeated; instead of it the two numbers of *Apparitions* appeared in their place and the first number of *Harmonies poétiques et religieuses* (both 1834) without opus number. Then the numbering was continued from 5 to 13 (with the omission of many words occurring between) and goes on up to the year 1838.

In 1837 the new edition of the twelve studies without opus number appeared almost at the same time in Paris, Vienna and Milan.

We can now compare the first setting with the second. The Liszt whom we meet here has shot up to an unexpected height. The boy of the first setting where awakening was still in the future is not recognisable in the wonderful youth. Apparently without transition, he surpassed all available and imaginable possibilities of the piano and he never made such an immeasurable stride again. It is true that later in his search for poetic transparent sounds and by using his resources more sparingly for effects aimed at more surely he climbed still higher—into an even more refined atmosphere—and it is only in the third period that the far more inner penetrating sweetness of his maturity is harvested. Finally, he arches the bridge to childhood by employing what is seemingly most spontaneous and what is deceivingly self-evident. A turning back which is not a going back; for the man stands in a different way on the same sure place of the bank, before and after he has crossed and recrossed the stream. The primitiveness in creation and form is of two different kinds. At first he learnt how to fill out and afterwards he learnt how to leave out.

The French, Austrian and Italian impressions of the second setting correspond with each other. They are divided into two parts and in France and Austria are dedicated to Czerny. But the Ricordi edition only dedicates the first part to his teacher, the second part Liszt (or the publisher?) dedicates "à Frederic Chopin." The Haslinger impression has this title:

24
Grandes Études
Pour le Piano
composées et dediées
À Monsieur Charles Czerny
par
F. Liszt
Vienne chez Tob. Haslinger

Always *twenty-four* while both the parts only contain twelve! Nothing followed in this plan either, and there were never more than twelve studies. Both the editions came into Robert Schumann's hands at the same moment; and he wrote about them in detail in his own *Neue Zeitschrift für Musik*, 1839 (Rob. Schumann, *Gesammelte Schriften über Musik und Musiker*, 2 Vols.). "Closer inspection proves then," he writes, "that most of the pieces of the later work are only a revision of that youthful work which had already appeared many, perhaps twenty years ago in Lyons." (We have learnt that they came out eleven years previously in Marseilles.) Schumann's comparison passes sentence unfavourably on the new version "where we are often uncertain whether we do not envy the boy more than the man, who seems unable to arrive at any peace!"

A *Davidsbündler* expects—demands—from one who is twenty-six years old, and above all from the twenty-six-year-old Liszt, that he should attain to peace!

In the renunciation of his opinions as a *Davidsbündler* Schumann goes still further, since from such accusations as "lack of study," the "backwardness of the composer compared with the virtuoso," and other criticisms, he draws the conclusion that it was "indeed too late" after the salutary meeting with Chopin "for the extraordinary virtuoso to make up for what he misses as a composer." With these and still sharper words Schumann represents the twenty-six-year-old Liszt in the full maturity of his powers who "with his eminently musical nature . . . should also have become an important composer" as someone hopeless, and at the same time unjustly forgets to think of his own late development.

Then Schumann proceeds to a comparison of the opening bars of different studies out of both editions. These examples, inscribed with "formerly" and "now," are chosen in an amateurish way, for it is not from the opening bars that the outward and inward growth of Liszt's gift are seen, but much more from the completely altered plan of many of these studies, and from the new spirit which blows through the later ones.

These examples from the first, fifth and ninth numbers are right in their numbering just as, on the whole, what Schumann says is right about the differences in the first five. But then he commits an obvious error if (with reference to the second edition) he is of the opinion that "the three that follow now are 'quite new', namely the numbers 6, 7 and 8." This is only applicable to the seventh which becomes the "Eroica" later. The source of the sixth and eighth is present—clearly!—in the corresponding numbers of the first version; and as he has already cited opening bars Schumann could have proved a connection between the introduction of the Impromptu, op. 3, and the introduction of the seventh, a connection which exists in reality.

No. 6 in the 1st version *(Molto agitato)*

No. 6 in the 2nd version *(Largo)*

No. 8 in the 1st version *(Allegro con spirito)*

No. 8 in the 2nd version *(Presto strepitoso)*

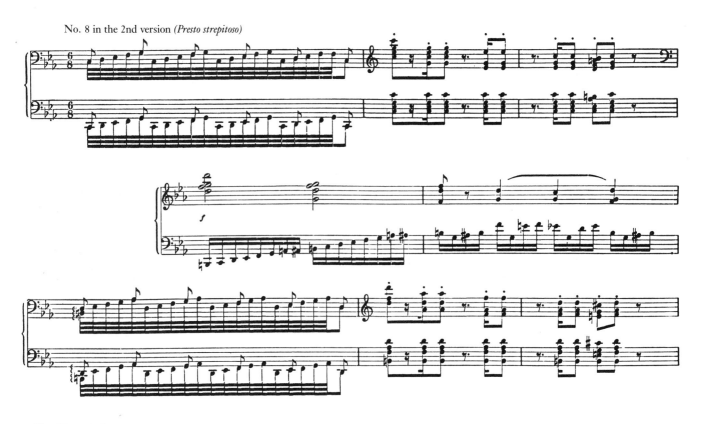

Introduzione.

Impromptu brillant, op. 3 *(Allegretto)*

Etude no. 7 in the 2nd version *(Allegro deciso)*

Largo.

smorz.

But in case the reader should perchance misunderstand him, Schumann comes back to this erroneous statement towards the end of his report. "Numbers 6, 8 and 11 of the Hofmeister edition are omitted in the new one (their places are taken by these three new ones); perhaps Liszt will bring them into the next volume for he will certainly work through the whole circle of keys." Schumann's report ends with the following major half close, which, to us, is more significant: "It was with these studies that he [Liszt] made such an amazing effect during his last visit to Vienna. But great results presume great causes, and an audience does not allow itself to be enthusiastic over nothing."

Between this second and the final third edition of the studies, there comes a rather different and enriched setting of the fourth study (in Paris with Maurice Schlesinger, later, with Haslinger in Vienna). In the French edition the five introductory bars added previously are reproduced on the first page in facsimile of Liszt's handwriting. Above them for the first time is the poetic title "Mazeppa" and to the right of them is a dedication—"à Victor Hugo"—otherwise "Mazeppa" coincides in text and in general conception with the fourth study and only at the end does the kingly D major flourish surprise us, which, still an embryonic formation, here was to become a separate part in the symphonic poem of the same name. The explanatory last line of the original poem is only brought in musically; the words "il tombe enfin . . . et se relève Roi!" were first introduced in the third complete edition.

This final third and most complete edition (published in 1852 by Breitkopf & Härtel) means for us the entire Liszt, for from now on technique goes side by side with the idea as assistant to it! Would that everyone who is not yet in touch with Liszt might above all be impressed with this fundamental thought.

With the exception of the seventh study ("Eroica"), which, to me, in the second setting has broader characteristics and more uniformity, all the studies find their irrevocable form here for the first time.

The final improvements in Liszt's compositions for the piano are to be found in a greater ease and smooth playableness and a corresponding amount of impressive effect and character. For instance the F minor study in the second setting presents almost insurmountable difficulties if the speed, the required fire in execution and the correct performance of details are taken into account. Apart from this tenth and the second study they all have *poetic titles*.

The "Preludio" is less a prelude to the cycle than a prelude to test the instrument and the disposition of the performer after stepping on to the concert platform. The next piece: one of those Paganini devilries similar to those in the *Fantaisie sur la Clochette* and the *Rondo Fantastique sur un Thème Espagnol*.

"Paysage": a calm renunciation of everything worldly—taking breath during the contemplation of nature, a self-contemplation but not quite without passion; this was only achieved completely by the later Liszt.

"Mazeppa": a symphonic poem for the pianoforte which has already been discussed.

In "Feux Follets" ornament is united with colour. Their combination, which reaches its summit in *Les Jeux d'Eau à la Villa d'Este* was not without influence in the origin of Wagner's *Waldweben* and *Feuerzauber*. (The "Catholic" Liszt perhaps exercised a still more forcible influence on his great friend, which was willingly admitted by Wagner and acknowledged in *Parsifal*.)

In "Vision" we may think—so we learn from the superscription—of the funeral of the first Napoleon, advancing with solemn and imperial pomp.

The "Eroica," more defiant than heroic, begins falteringly, then sweeps up to a climax, which has all the characteristics of Liszt's brilliance.

"Wilde Jagd" displays the strongest orchestral colouring—and there is in it, as in the *Dante* Sonata, a foundation for the symphonic poem as it was realised in César Franck's *Chasseur Maudit*.

"Ricordanza" gives the impression of a bundle of faded love letters from a somewhat old-fashioned world of sentiment.

The title "Appassionata" would well suit the following F minor Study and the whole bell-like magic of the pianoforte extends with flattering and impetuous charm over *Harmonies du Soir*.

"Chasse-neige," the noblest example, perhaps, amongst all music of a poetising nature—a sublime and steady fall of snow which gradually buries landscape and people.

(b) *The Paganini Studies*

The first and second editions of the Paganini Studies run concurrently with the second and third of the Great Studies.

1837 Second edition of the Studies
1838 First edition of the Paganini Studies
1852 Third edition of the Studies
1851 Second edition of the Paganini Studies

Instead of being based on his childhood's work as was the case with the Great Studies, the Paganini Studies are altogether original.

The genealogy would be incomplete, however, without adding the immediate successor of the Paganini Studies, and the ancestor of the third study. I mean the *Grande Fantaisie de Bravoure sur la Clochette de Paganini* published in 1834 in Paris and (later?) by Mechetti in Vienna with the opus number 2. It is composed of a free, slow introduction, a capricious fleeting anticipation of thematic material, leading up to a connecting sentence which is brought to a climax by the most daring bravura; the theme, a *Variation à la Paganini* and a *Finale de Bravura*. The care, choice and minuteness of detail given to the directions for performance in these most youthful pieces by Liszt (like *Apparitions*, *Harmonies poétiques*, *Fantaisie Romantique Suisse*, etc.) leave almost no doubt regarding the pianist-composer's intentions. The method for their execution is marked out step by step and suggestions are even made for the purely pianistic performance (as for example: "Marquez les 6 temps de la mesure en jetant la main avec souplesse"). For this reason they are worth the closest attention and are instructive for the Liszt style. The work itself, in spite of many abnormalities, is penetrated with an unusual spirit, a strangely oppressed feeling, struggling for expression. The series of Paganini Studies follows it, of which the third takes up the bell-like motive again, whilst the remaining five are taken from the Violin Caprices. The Vienna publication of Haslinger gives them their titles in two languages:

Études
d'Exécution Transcendante
d'après Paganini
Bravour-Studien
nach
Paganini Capricen
für das Pianoforte bearbeitet
und der
Frau Clara Schumann geborenen Wieck
K. K. Kammervirtuosin
gewidmet
von
F. Liszt

As a kind of homage to Clara's husband (worldly-wise or a Mephistophelian whim?) over the first of these studies is printed Liszt's predecessor's treatment of it: "Cette seconde version est celle de Mr. Robert Schumann."

There are in existence two different versions by Liszt of the fourth study, so both volumes really contain eight altogether instead of six studies.

The manner of transcription has the true Paganini *diablerie*, "of such a kind," remarks the critic Schumann, "as may even cost Liszt some study. Whoever masters these variations (Study No. 6) as they should be mastered, in any easy, entertaining way, so that they glide past us like different scenes in a marionette show, may travel confidently all over the world and will return with golden laurels, a second Paganini-Liszt."

Clearly conscious of the hint contained in this sentence, a second transcription was made by Liszt—twelve years later—in which the obvious aim—namely "the easy entertaining manner of a marionette show" became practicable. The result of a comparison of both these editions is almost richer in disclosures than in that of the Great Studies. The way in which simplification and concentration are poured together produces "slickness" as though by a conjuring trick. Thus we see the fourth study in the second edition reduced from a previous four- and six-voice part to a one-voice part, the notes of which are restricted to one stave.

"La Campanella," the third study, has become quite unified in "one throw" here (it is difficult to believe very much in "throws"; this one lasted from the year 1834 to 1851!).

With the exception of "La Campanella" the studies bear no explanatory titles. Only to violinists the fifth is well known as "La Chasse." Without hesitation one can call the first "Il Tremolo" and the second—after the tempo prescribed—"Andante Capriccioso." The fourth, "Arpeggio," and the last "Tema e Variazioni."

(c) *Ab-irato* (d) *Trois Études de Concert*
(e) *Waldesrauschen and Gnomenreigen.*

A new link in the chain of studies appeared in 1840 under the ceremonious and yet in no way suitable title *Morceau de Salon: Étude de Perfectionnement de la Méthode des Méthodes* (an educational work published by Moscheles and Fétis).

This fruitful year saw the completion of Schubert's *Winterreise*, the publication of the *Sonnambula* Fantasy, the *Rákoczy* March, the first attempt at the Hungarian Rhapsodies (*Magyar Dallók*), and also the first transcription of the Mendelssohn and Beethoven songs, and the pianoforte score of the Beethoven Septet.

The study *Morceau de Salon*, etc., appeared revised in 1852, at a time when Liszt sorted and put in order his pianoforte compositions, gathering them together almost as if they were his last Will and Testament. In the new edition it was called *Ab-irato* and like its elder sister was published by Schlesinger in Berlin.

The three *Études de Concert* came out (1848) before this revision, and they bear throughout no revolutionary physiognomy (with the exception of the date); the Paris edition, otherwise unchanged, christened them *Caprices Poétiques* and named them successively and separately "Il lamento," "La leggierezza," "Un sospiro." Liszt's latest work of the species are the two *Études de Concert*, "Waldesrauschen" and "Gnomenreigen," composed for the Lebert and Stark (Cotta) school of pianoforte playing and incorporated in the same in 1863. They were published independently by Bahns Verlag in 1869.

In spite of taking all possible trouble I have, unfortunately, not been able to establish successfully whether or not differences exist in the publications of 1863 and 1869, as neither the firm of the Cotta edition, nor the K. Bibliothek in Berlin, nor the Liszt Museum in Weimar, nor I myself, possesses the first publications.

From the material in the six studies last discussed, one must conclude that Liszt had not exhausted himself with the very extended work on the Great Studies and the Paganini Studies, but yet had come to the end of this subject. This meant that he was relieved of an important task, while the stragglers were more like the children of mood and opportunity. Who would like to miss them? Not we who wish to preserve in this collective edition Liszt's smallest variations as he wrote them sometimes in a pupil's book. For, with a phenomenon that digresses and changes so much from the rule as that of Franz Liszt, it is often the fleeting idea seized by chance which is the characteristic one, and once vanished—it cannot be recaptured.

Berlin, 1910   Ferruccio Busoni

Editorial Notes

Etude en 12 Exercices

The Hofmeister edition serves as the basic source (compare the Foreword).

Page 1   1) This slur—lacking at the parallel passage—could be questioned.

"   2) In the original French edition, which we have referred to for comparison, the *fp* appears on the second eighth-note.

Page 2   3) In the Hofmeister edition, the octave symbol begins at the first sixteenth-note; however, the figure jumps to the higher octave only on the second sixteenth-note.

Page 3   4) *Allegro con moto* in the French edition.

"   5) *legero* (rather than the correct "leggiero") in the French edition.

"   6) No ♮ by the F in the French edition.

"   7) The *forte* symbol on the last eighth-note seems unmotivated.

"   8) Whether the fingering 4 3 2 should be repeated twice is questionable.

"   9) The first chord in the left hand is obviously meant to read:

"   10) Apparently a misunderstanding by the engraver. The figure should consist of three-note eighths:

Page 5   11) *ff* in the French edition.

Page 6   12) In the French edition the second quarter-note in the right hand appears as:

"   13) *p* in the French edition.

"   14) The French edition has:

Page 6   15) D = dotted quarter-note in the French edition.

"   16) The French edition has:

"   17) The French edition has:

The ♮ by the E is lacking in both editions.

"   18) In both editions, an accent ➤ on the third quarter-note, between the two inner voices; it is unclear for which of the two the sign is intended.

Page 7   19) This bar in the French edition:

"   20) In the French edition, no third, only G.

"   21)  , (French edition).

"   22) ▬ , (French edition).

"   23) The decrescendo symbol ➤ appears in the French edition.

Page 8   24) *sf* (in the French edition).

"   25) The ♯ by the G is lacking in the Hofmeister edition.

Page 9   26) In the French edition the slurs are missing; instead, there are staccato points over the higher three double notes.

Page 11   27) *p* in the French edition.

"   28) *dimin.* in the French edition.

Page 12   29) *cresc.* in the French edition.

Page 14   30) In the original, an E♭ appears here; obviously an engraver's error.

Page 15   31) In the original, B♭ here instead of G.

"   32) ◁ in the French edition.

"   33) The French edition has B♭ instead of C.

Page 16 34) in the French edition.

" 35) *ten.* (in the French edition).

" 36) The ♮ by the G is lacking in the original. We assume this is an oversight.

Page 18 37) The *piano* indication contradicts the mood of the whole piece. We have added the more plausible *f* in parentheses.

Page 19 38) In the French edition, the fourth quarter-note in the right hand reads .

It is more correct and corresponds to the subsequent parallel passage.

Page 21 39) In the French edition a ♮ appears by the .

" 40) The slur is missing in the Hofmeister edition.

" 41) *espressivo* similarly missing.

" 42) In the French edition the slur begins over the third quarter-note.

" 43) In the French edition *sf* appears instead of *f*.

Page 22 44) *cresc.* in the French edition.

" 45) in the French edition.

" 46) The ♭ is missing by the G in the whole bar and in all editions.

Page 27 47) In the French edition:

Page 28 48) D♯ is dubious. The French edition omits it.

" 49) Both editions omit the slurs on the second quarter-note. In the French edition, they are also missing in the next bar and on the last quarter-note of the bar following.

Page 29 50) The French edition has here C instead of B♭.

" 51) in the French edition.

Page 31 52) The ♮ by the G is missing in both editions.

" 53) The French edition gives the last quarter-note as follows:

" 54) In the French edition, A♭ (rather than F) on the last eighth-note.

Page 32 55) The third quarter-note reads

in the French edition; that is, with the first F held and a breath mark before the fourth quarter-note, with which the primary motive reenters.

" 56) In the original, D♭ appears here instead of B♭.

12 Grandes Etudes

As primary source we used the Haslinger edition and compared it with the Paris edition of Schlesinger. The engravers' errors of both largely canceled each other out; however, where small uncertainties and obvious errors still remained, we have—for the sake of the larger overall view—included them or their corrections in parentheses, either in the music itself or above it. Similarly, we have inserted a few small critical notes.

Etudes d'Exécution Transcendante

Source: *Etudes d'exécution transcendante*, Cahier I et II. (Leipzig, Breitkopf & Härtel.)

The metronome markings are intended to indicate only the approximate tempo of the beginning.

Page 158 As regards the variants for 7-octave piano mentioned here and later, these variants can be used with the extended range of our modern pianos.

" 158 For the dates of composition, see the Foreword.

" 159 1st staff, upbeat. The *f* does not appear in the primary source.

" 171 3rd staff. In this case, it seems artistically advisable to reserve the amplified version over the second bar for the repeat of the passage (p. 176). The form of the second amplified version shows that in the first case the continuation in the main text should begin with the eighth note of the second bar of the third staff.

" 174 1st staff, 1st bar. In the old edition appears the marking *un poco animato*, with which instruction the editor agrees. To be played with restrained passion.

" 176 5th staff, 1st bar. The sudden *mp*, which alone makes a broader crescendo possible, should be observed.

" 180 3rd staff, 1st, 2nd and 3rd bars. The source is rhythmically unclear here. Presumably the melody in the bass and inner voices should go:

3 dots 3 dots 2 dots

Page 182 4th staff, 1st bar. For the sixth 32nd-note in the right hand, the source has a ♮ by the A. Apparently it should appear by the G. (Resolution of G♭. See also left hand.)

" 197 1st staff, 2nd bar. The first double note of the right hand is

in the source instead of the correct

" 200 Compare the note (with musical example) referring to the Eroica etude in the Foreword.

" 205 3rd staff, 1st and 2nd bars. The legato slurs were added by the editor. Compare the Prelude to the *Carnival at Pest*.

" 223 3rd staff, 1st bar. The trill on E must presumably be performed with the upper auxiliary F, that on E♯ with the upper auxiliary F♯.

" 227 Ramann's *Liszt-Pädagogium* provides, after the 4th staff, the following extension of the ending, which is recommended:

Page 243 1st staff, 2nd bar. In the source, the third quarter-note of the melody reads: . The lower A♭ is, by analogy with the foregoing, an engraver's error and should be a C, to which it has accordingly been changed.

" 247 2nd staff, 1st bar ff. The tremolo always in the character of the beginning *(non martellato)*: suspended, whispered, rustling.

" 252 4th staff. The notation of the last seven notes as 32nd-notes indicates a possible *allargando* and *meno legato*.

In the critical review of the engraved source, Professor Otto Taubmann was of kind assistance.

Etude en 12 Exercices
Etude in 12 Exercises
Op. 1
1.

2.

⁴⁾ **Allegro non molto.** M. ♩ = 100.

3.

Allegro sempre legato. M. ♩ = 80

dimin.

ritard.

4.

Allegretto. M. ♩.= 132.

6.

Molto agitato. M. ♩ = 138.

30)

7.

Allegretto con molta espressione. M. ♩ = 96.

8.

Allegro con spirito. ♩=88.

37) *p(f)*

9.

Allegro grazioso. M. $\quad$ = 160.

10.

Moderato. M. ♩ = 96.

11.

Allegro grazioso. M. ♩=92.

12.

Allegro non troppo. M. ♩ = 92.

12 Grandes Etudes
12 Large Etudes

1.

3.

Presto agitato assai.

sf

sempre più forte ed appassionato

sf *sf* *sf* *sf*

8······

sf *sf* *sf* *sf* *p*

8······

subito *più crescendo* *ff* *fff*

8······

poco a poco diminuendo e rallentando

4.

Allegro patetico.

espressivo e un poco marcato il canto

l'accompagnamento piano e leggiero

oppure:

poco a poco

cresc.

più cresc.

5.

rechte Hand
main droite
right hand

leggiero

p sotto voce

ben pronunziato ed espressivo il canto

3 2 1 2

Ossia.

rinf.

7.

Allegro deciso.

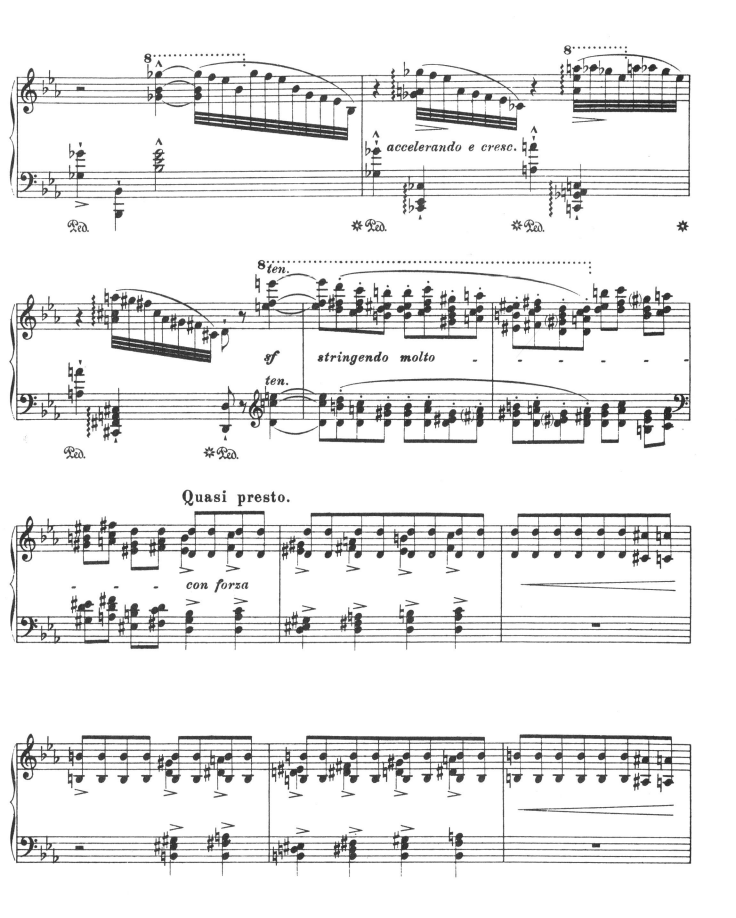

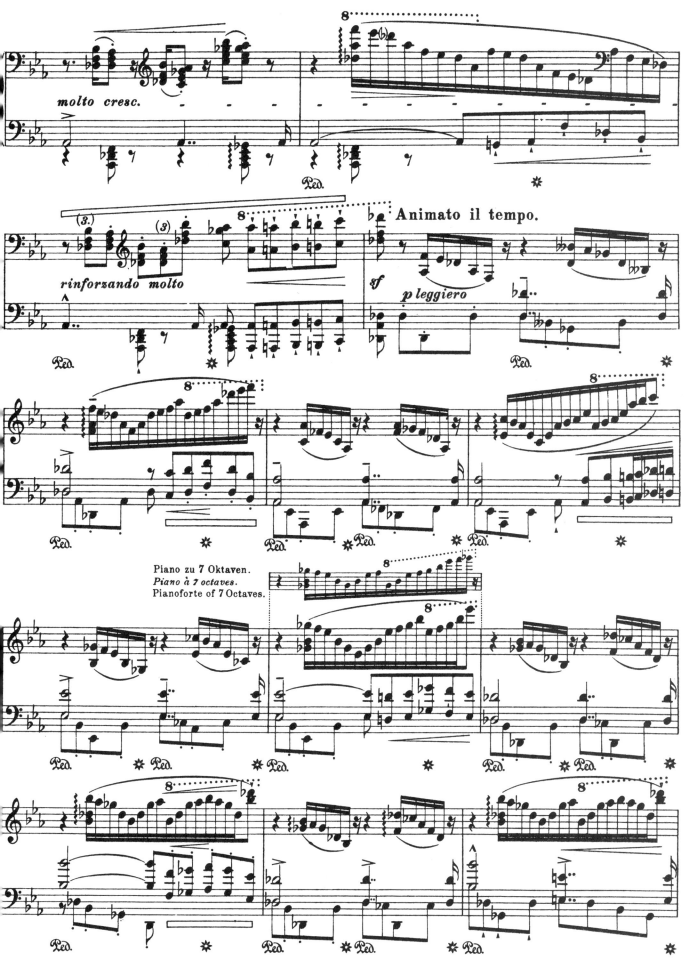

Piano zu 7 Oktaven.
Piano à 7 octaves.
Pianoforte of 7 Octaves.

Più animato ancora.

sempre *ff fuocoso*

Piano zu **7** Oktaven.
Piano à 7 octaves.
Pianoforte of **7** Octaves.

8.

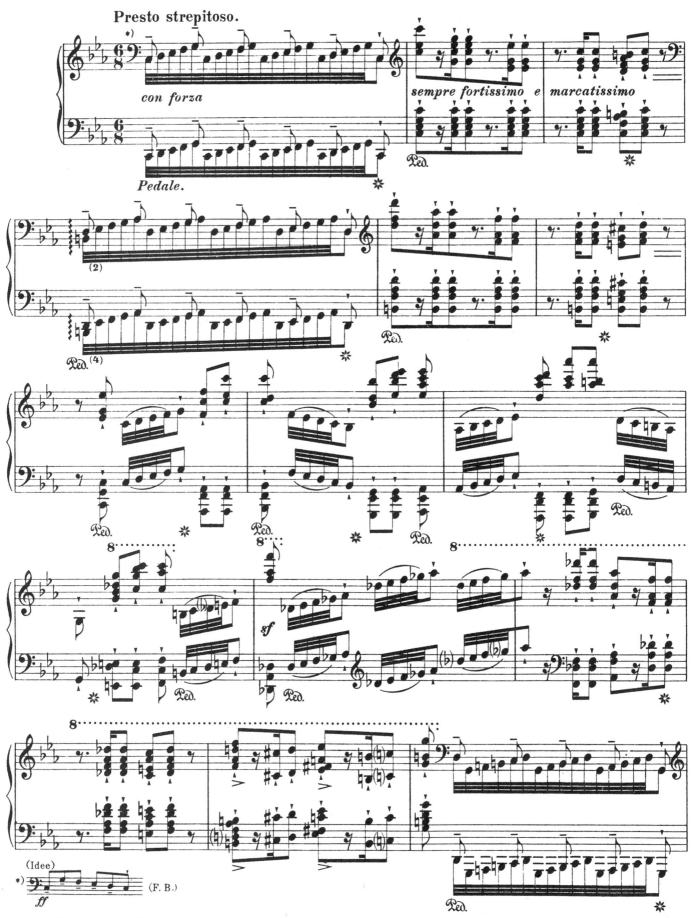

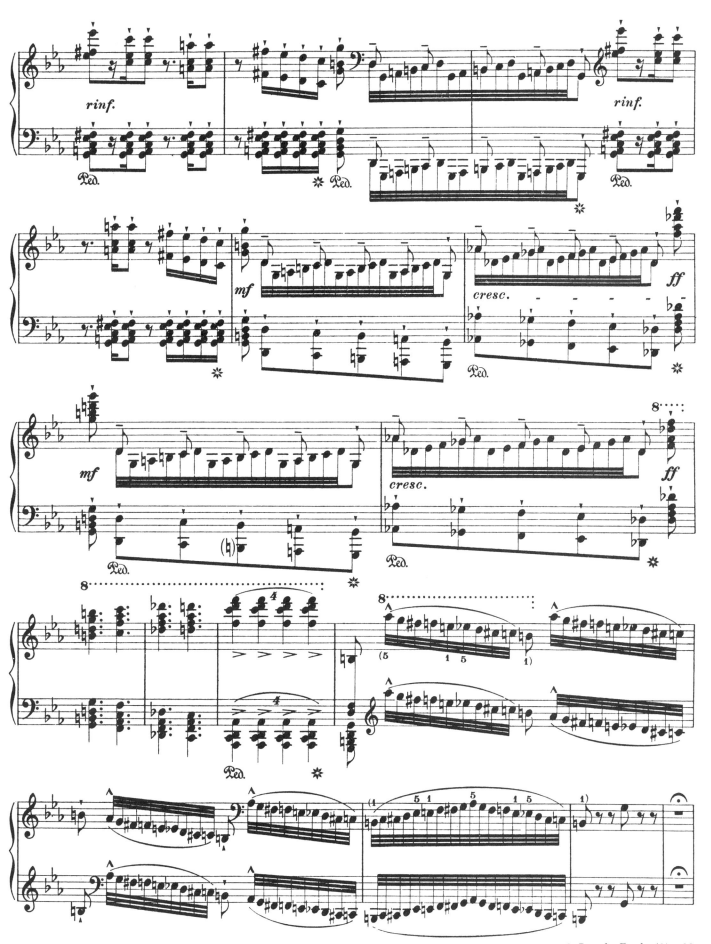

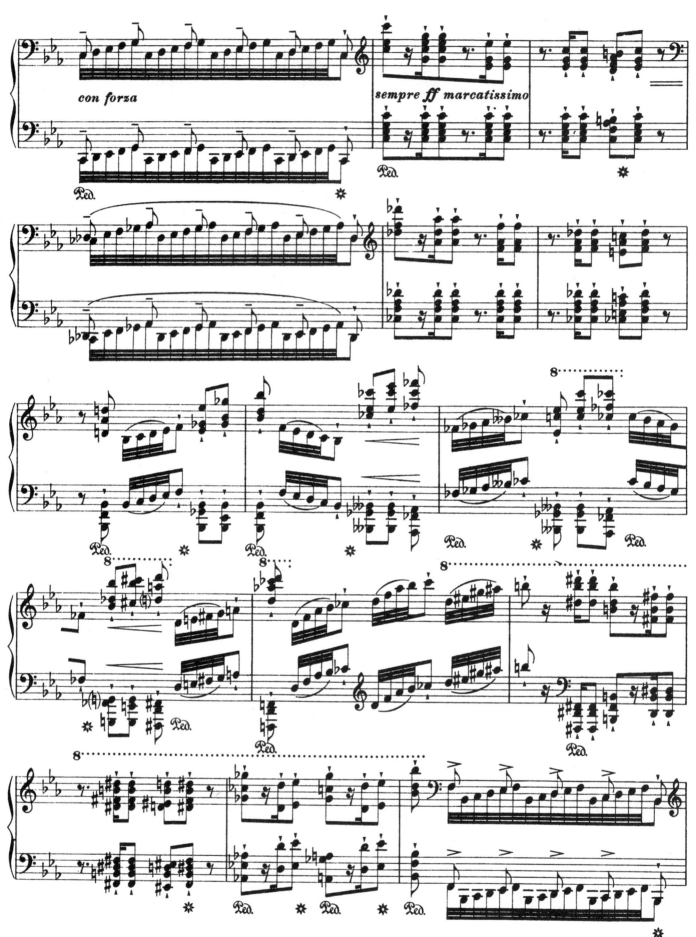

9.

accelerando e molto crescendo _ _ _ _ rinf. velocissimo

dimin. leggierissimo   pp

ppp   pppp   ritard.   lunga pausa

Tempo rubato.   ten.   ten.

dolce con grazia

cresc.

*) Die Triole ist offenbar so gemeint:
   Evidemment le triolet doit être entendu comme suit: (F. B.)
   The triplet is evidently meant as follows:

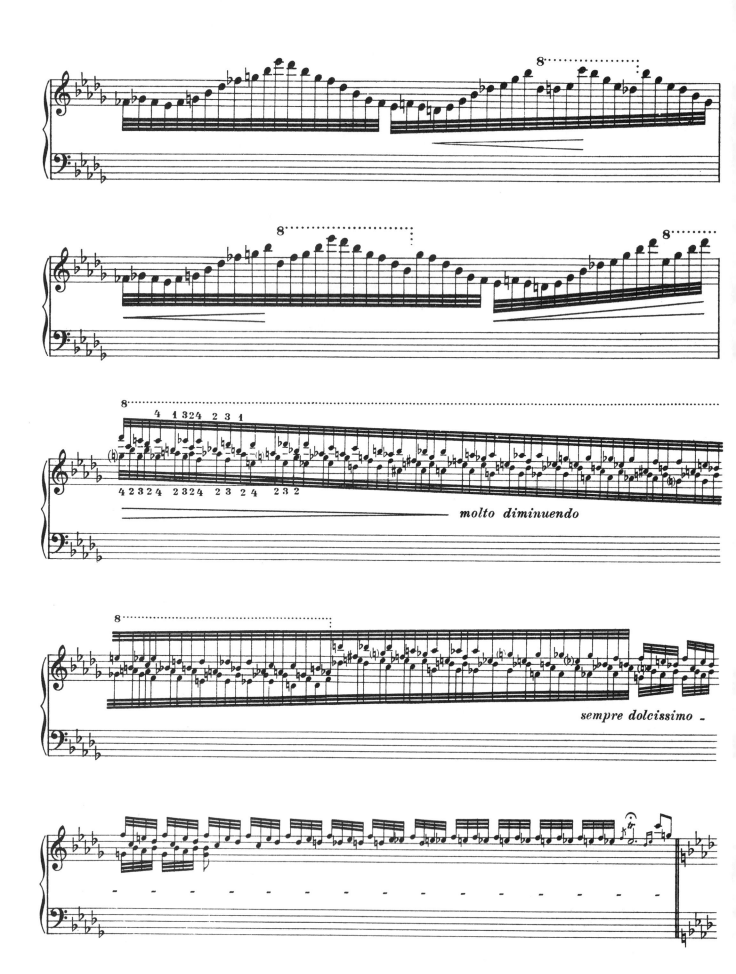

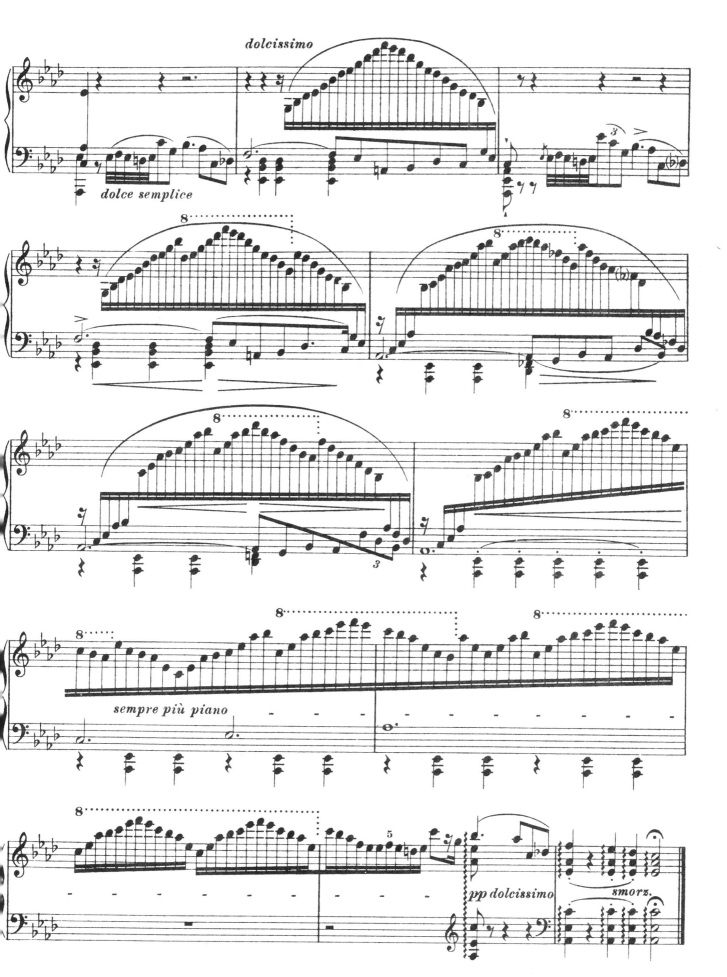

10.

Presto molto agitato.

Prestissimo agitato ed appassionato assai.

) (Tempo rubato.)

molto espressivo il canto

gli accompagnamenti sempre dolce

sempre staccato

poco rinf.

più rinf.

cresc.

f con passione

ancora più appassionato

poco riten.

) Während dieser ganzen Seite muß man die größte Sorgfalt darauf verwenden, die Rhythmen der Begleitungen der rechten Hand nicht
mit denen der linken Hand zu vermengen und die Achtelbewegung von jener der Triolen scharf zu trennen.

*Dans toute cette page, il faut mettre le plus grand soin à ne pas confondre les rythmes des accompagnements de la main droite avec
ceux de la main gauche, et distinguer nettement le mouvement des croches de celui des triolets.*

For the whole page the greatest care must be taken not to confound the rhythms of the accompaniments for the right hand with
those for the left hand, and distinguish clearly the quaver movement from the triplet movement.

12 Grandes Etudes (11)   131

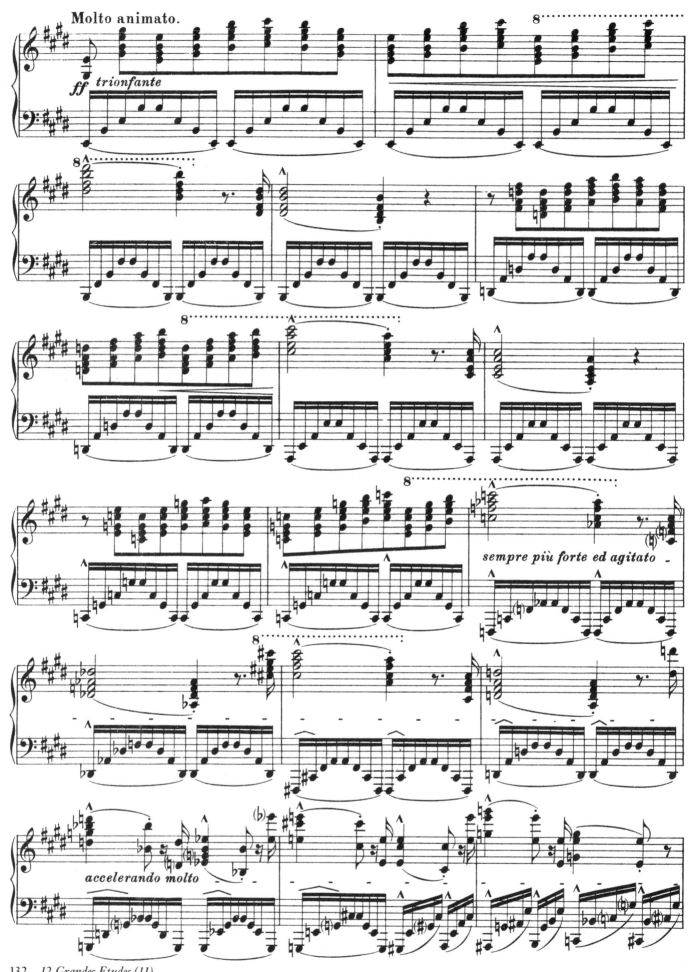

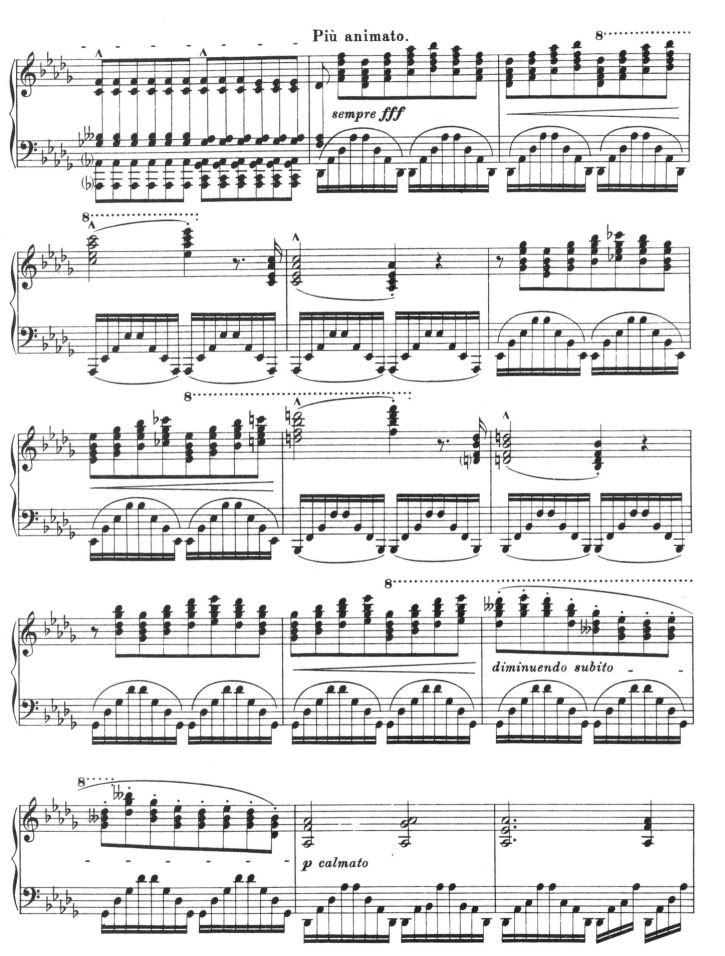

12.

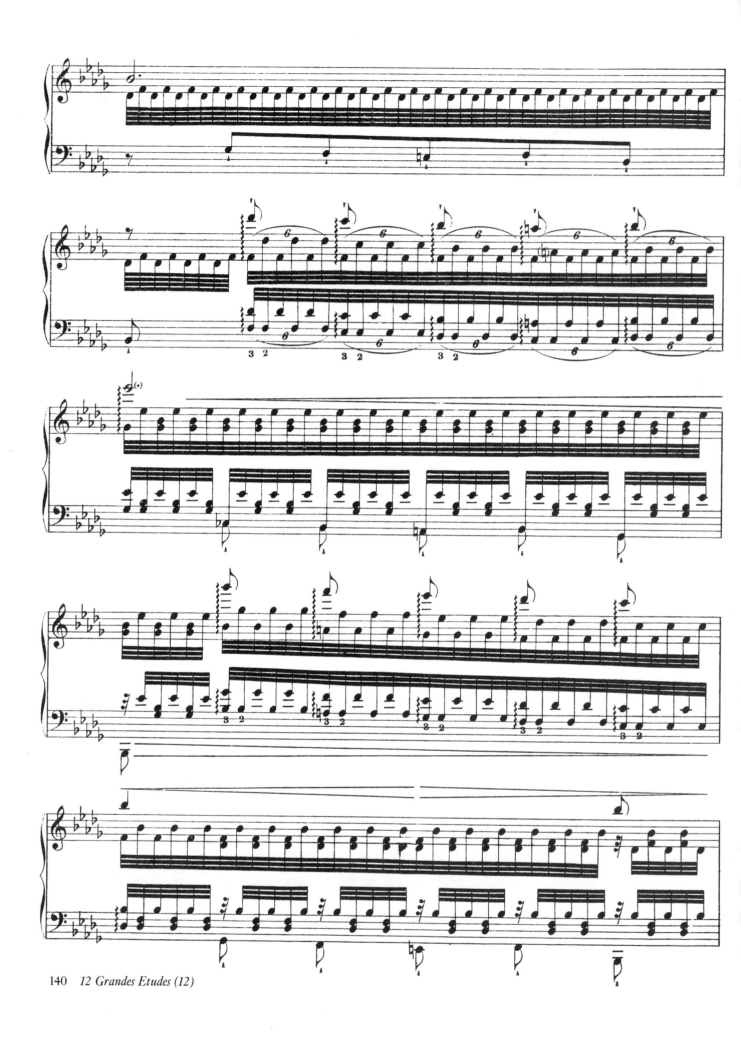

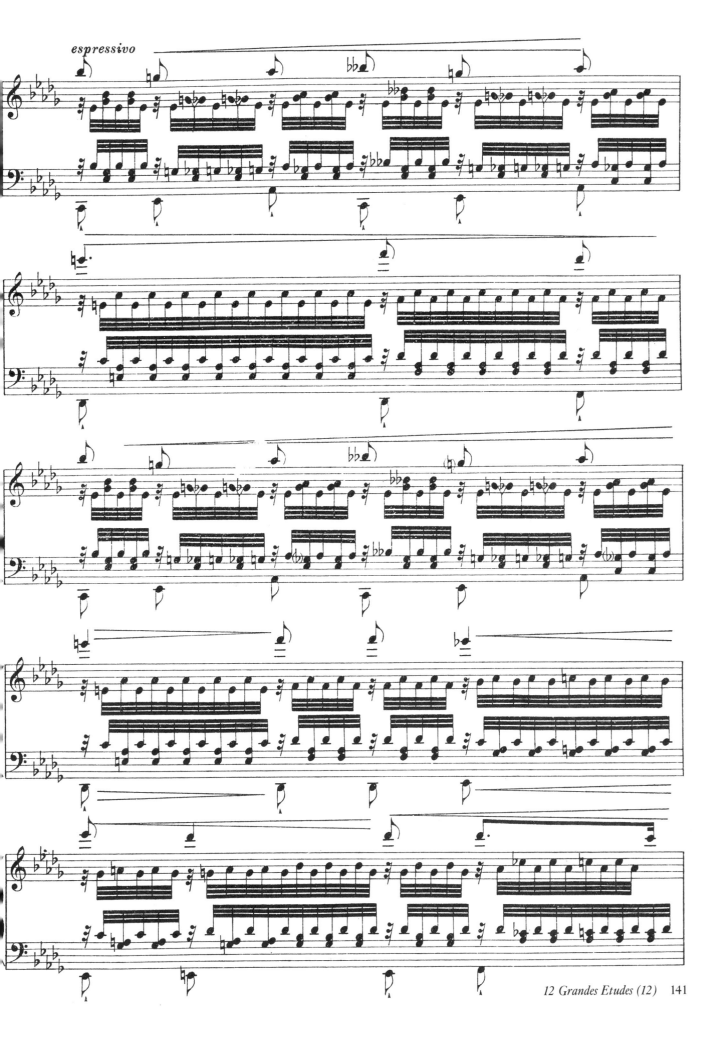

Mazeppa

Piano zu **7** Oktaven.
*Piano à **7** octaves.*
Pianoforte of **7** Octaves.

accelerando

sempre più forte

tumultuoso

simile

fff staccato, con bravura

ancora più cresc.

*) Diese sechs Noten fast zusammen.
Ces six notes presque ensemble.
The six notes almost simultaneously.

156 *Mazeppa*

Etudes d'Exécution Transcendante
Transcendental Etudes
1.
Preludio

2.

3.

Paysage

Un poco più animato il tempo.

4.

Mazeppa

Piano zu 7 Oktaven.
Piano à 7 octaves.
Pianoforte of 7 Octaves.

il più forte possibile

poco rallent.

Allegro deciso.

ff

crescendo

rinforzando assai

Più Moderato.
(*non piano*)

(*più p*)

(*pp*)

rall.

Vivace.

ten.

8ᵃ bassa...

«Il tombe enfin!... et se relève Roi!»
(Victor Hugo.)
"He falls at last . . . and rises as a king!"

5.

Feux Follets

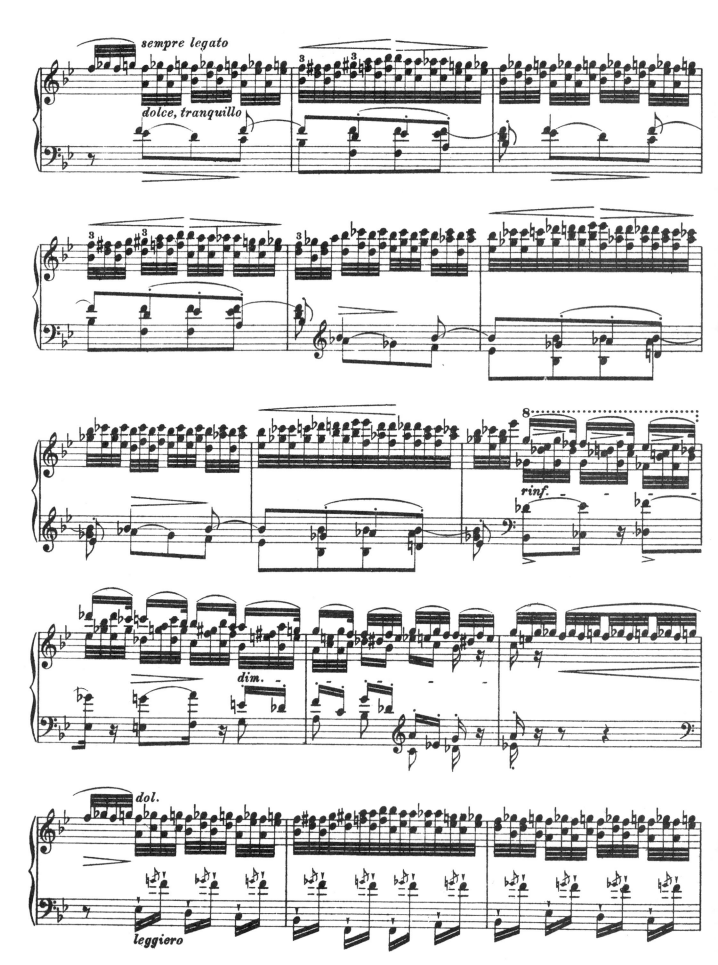

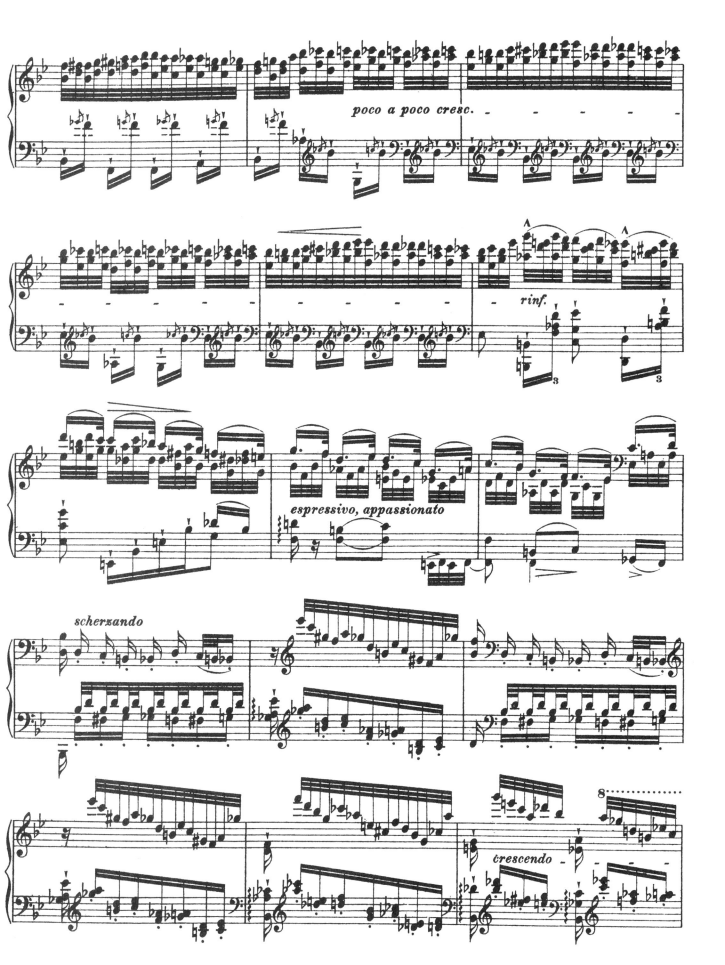

186   *Etudes d'Exécution Transcendante (5: Feux Follets)*

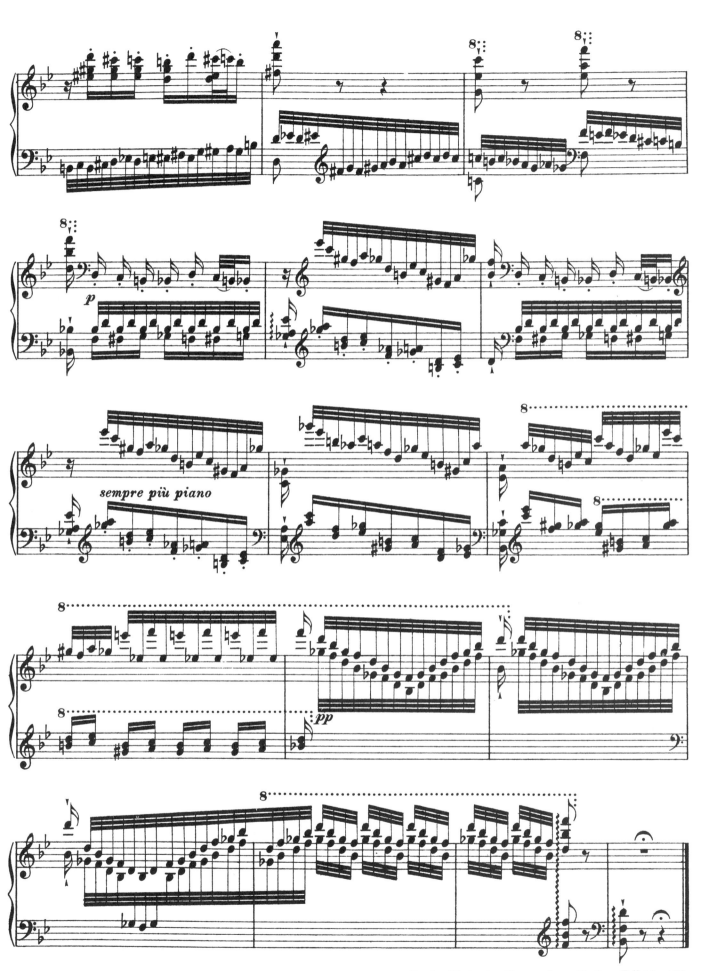

6

Vision

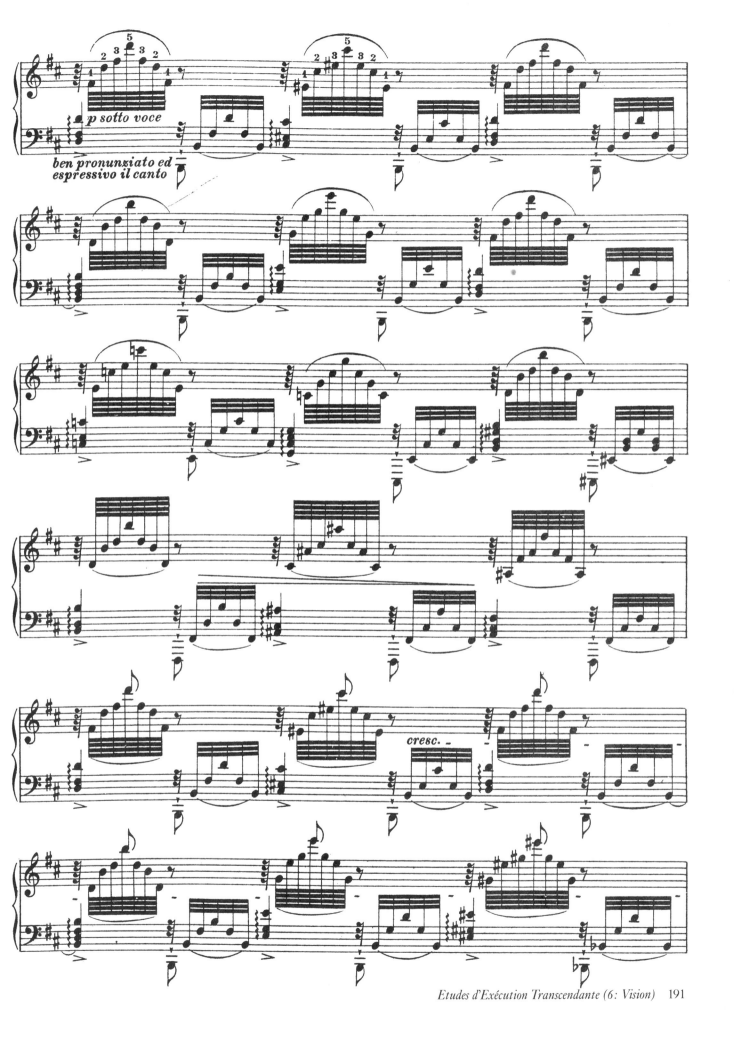

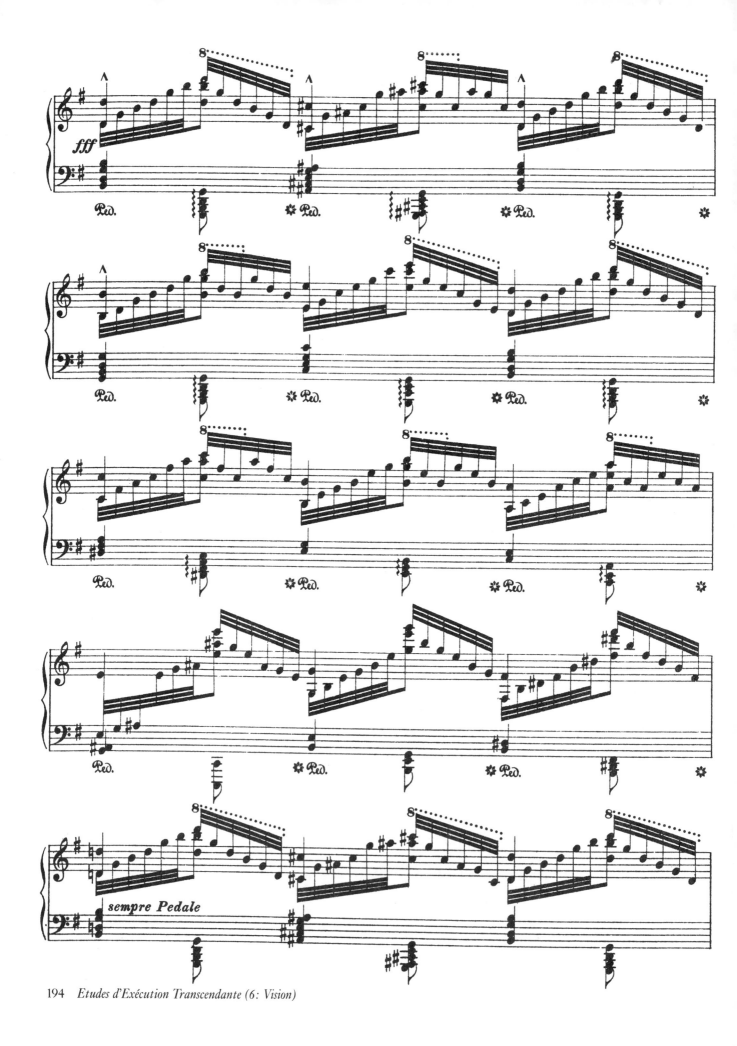

meno forte ma sempre espress.

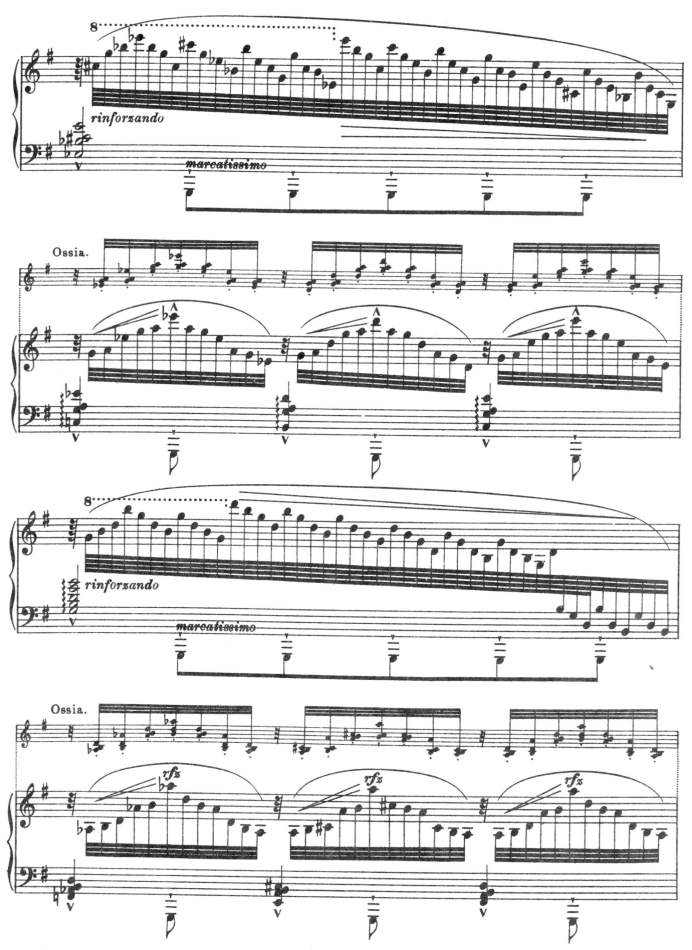

7.
Eroica

sempre marcato il canto e piani gli accompagnamenti

poco a poco cresc.

più cresc.

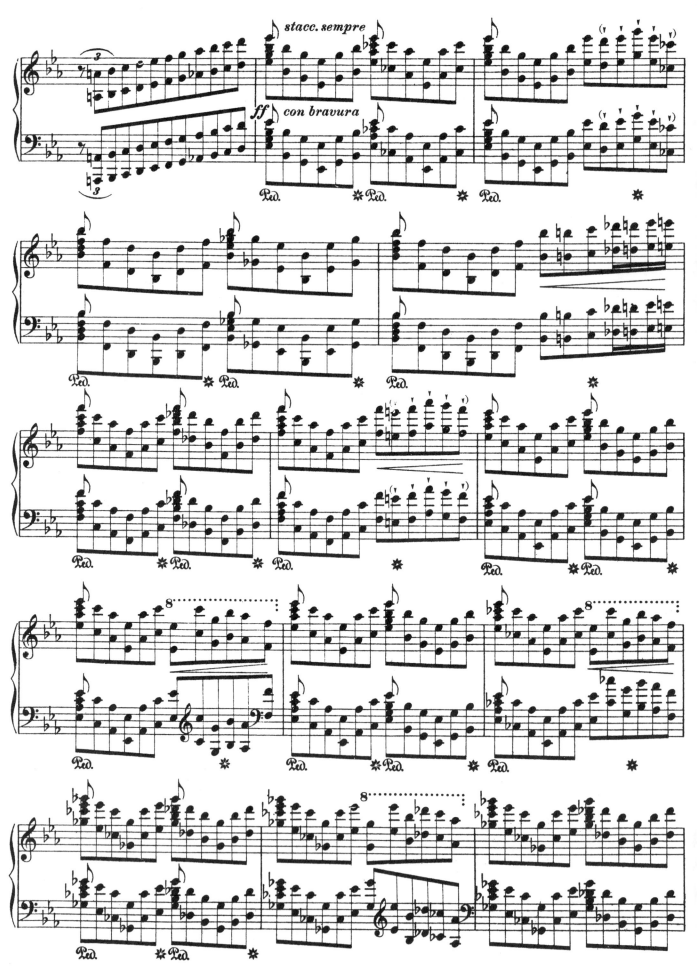

8.
Wilde Jagd

9

Ricordanza

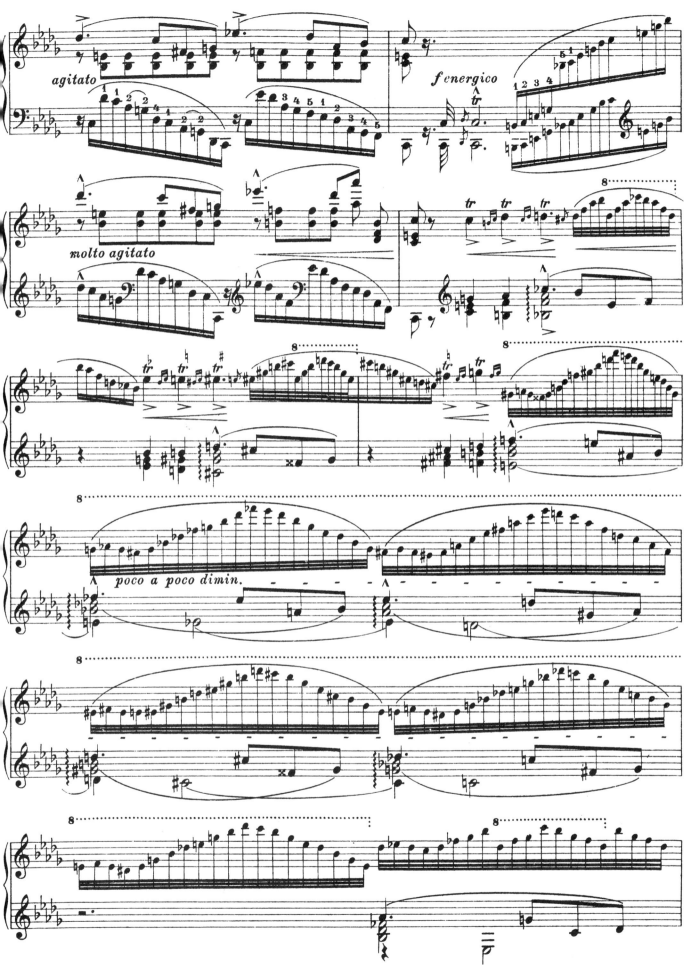

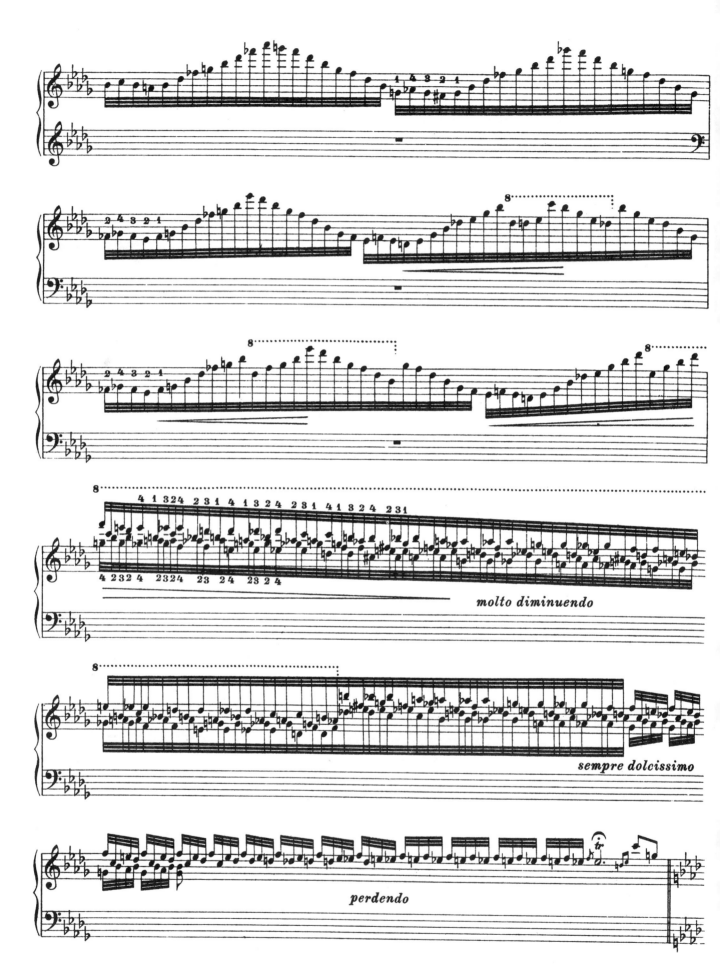

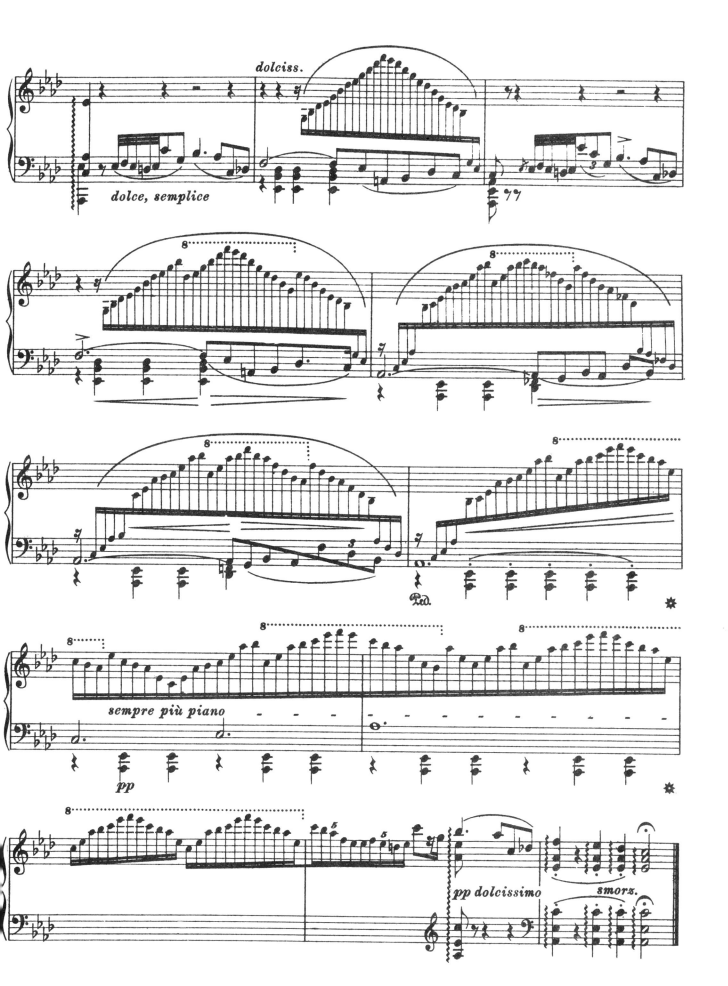

10.

accentato ed appassionato

11.

Harmonies du Soir

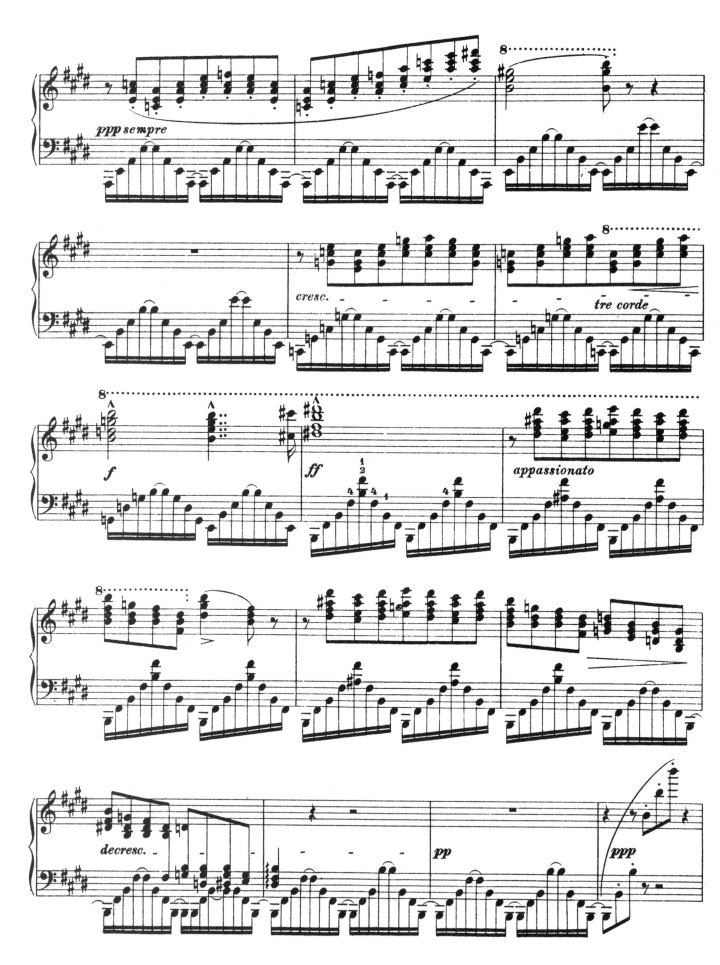

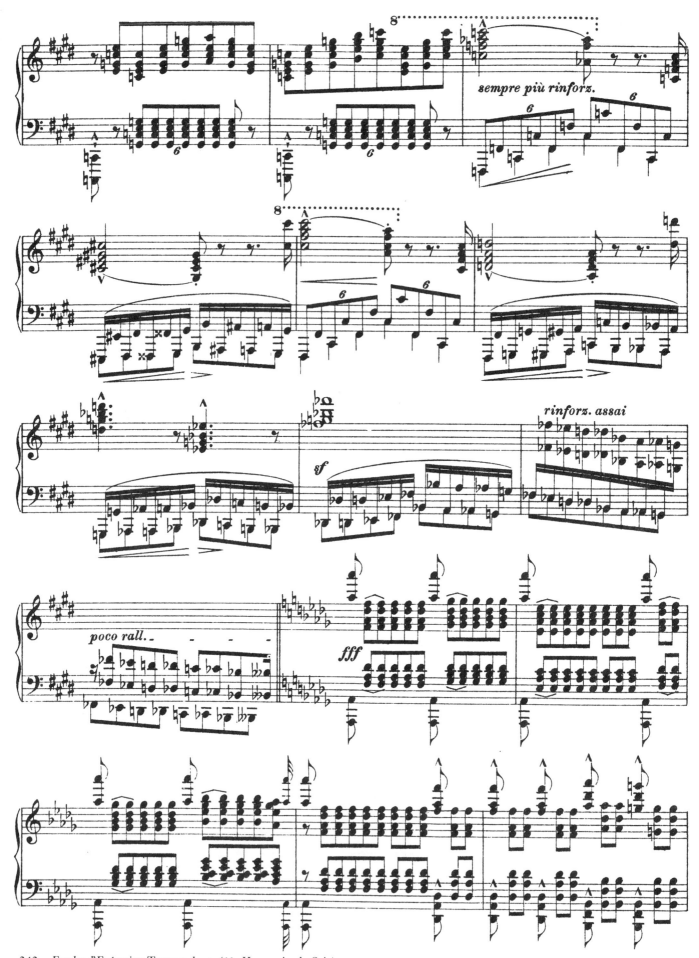

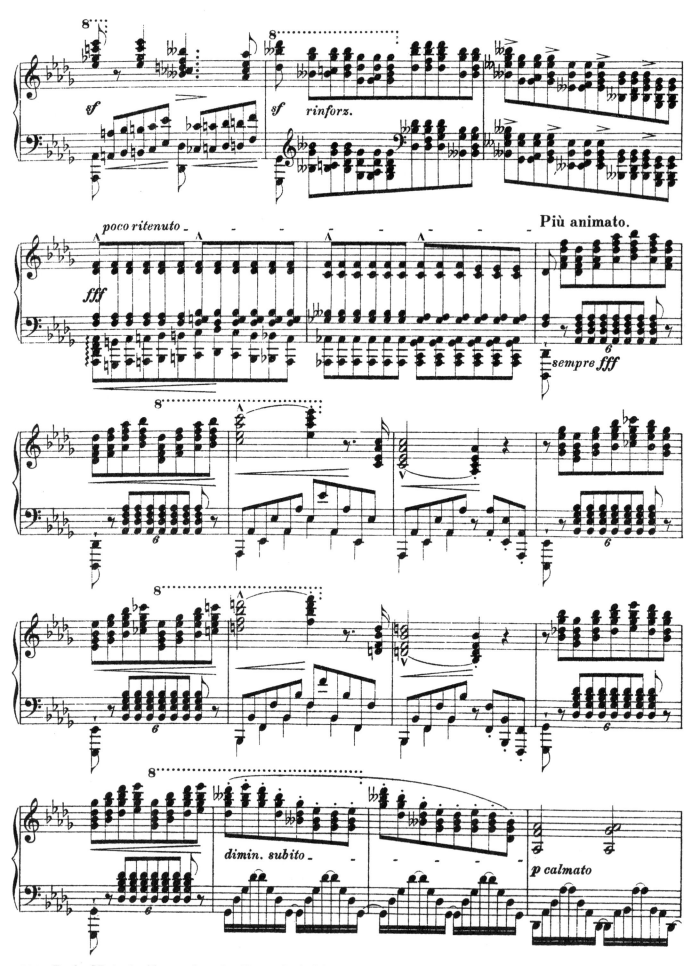

12.

Chasse-Neige

Andante con moto ($\flat$=100).

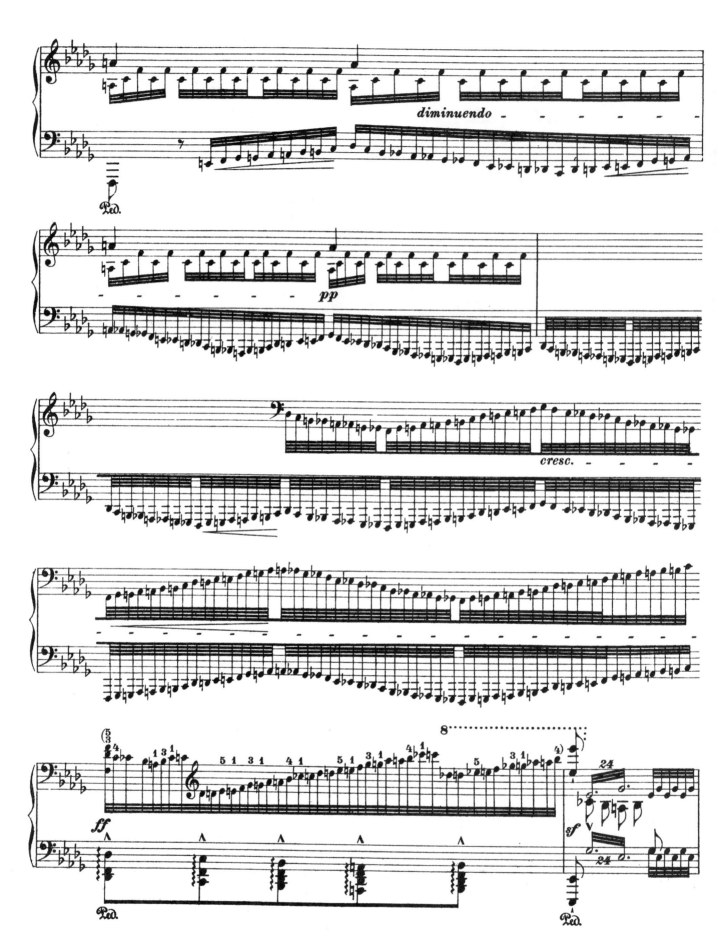